Little People, **BIG DREAMS**™

HANS CHRISTIAN ANDERSEN

Written by
Maria Isabel Sánchez Vegara

Illustrated by
Maxine Lee-Mackie

Frances Lincoln
Children's Books

Little Hans was born in a small town in the Kingdom of Denmark. His family was very poor and could barely afford a roof over their heads. But they had one precious jewel that they kept carefully in the cupboard: a book.

Flying carpets, Arabian princesses, genies coming out of lamps… Every night, Hans would listen to his father's readings, and once he fell asleep, all he dreamed of was being the hero of these wonderful fairytales.

He was eager to learn how to read and went to school for some time. But when his father passed away, Hans had to quit and take a job as a weaver's apprentice. It was not the exciting life he had imagined…

Still, one of his favorite hobbies was getting lost in the streets looking for puppeteers. Watching them was his greatest joy!

He would memorize each word and gesture, and repeat it later for his only audience: his mom.

Willing to make a living as an artist, Hans jumped
on a carriage to Copenhagen—the big city—where
he joined the Royal Danish Theater.

Hans tried everything: acting, singing, dancing…
but all he got was a role as a troll.

Locked in his tiny room, waiting for someone to offer him another role, Hans spent his free time writing. One day, he showed one of his stories to the theater director. It was full of misspellings, but he found it just delightful.

Hans didn't earn any money from that first story, but something better: a chance to go back to school and learn to write Danish properly. He was the oldest student in his class, but he knew it's never too late if you really want to learn.

After graduating, Hans felt confident enough to write
whatever came into his mind: from a sad poem about
a candle that no-one loved, to the fantastic travelogues
of a man who even met talking cats.

He was making a living as an author when he met a charming young woman named Riborg. Hans fell deeply in love and was about to tell her when he got some terrible news: Riborg was getting married to another man.

Instead of hiding his feelings, Hans decided to put them down on paper and wrote some of the most beautiful fairy tales. There were stories of mermaids falling in love with princes, and ducklings dreaming of becoming swans.

His tales became so popular that, every night, kids all over Europe read them. But they were not just the children's favorites, grown-ups loved them, too! And they all kept Hans's books like treasures, just like he used to do.

The stories lived forever, not only in books but in plays, ballets, and movies. But Hans's highest honor was that every second of April—the day of his birthday—kids all over the world now celebrate Children's Book Day.

By never hiding his feelings and letting his imagination fly, little Hans got what he had longed for: being loved. Not just by one single person, but by entire generations of children who know there is a swan inside each of us.

HANS CHRISTIAN ANDERSEN

(Born 1805 • Died 1875)

1836

1845

Hans Christian Andersen was born in Odense, Denmark, in 1805. His family didn't have much money, but his parents always made sure to encourage his interests and curiosity. At home, he played all the different parts he had seen on stage at the theater where his mother worked. It was clear he had a bright and unique imagination. Despite his family's difficulties, he became determined to make it as a star in the theater. So, one day, he headed for Copenhagen, Denmark's capital—by stowing away on a mail wagon. There, he took lessons in performing, but found his true love was writing. After some years struggling to get noticed, he published his first collection of fairy tales, and something magical started to happen. When people read Hans's stories, they felt like they were hearing them out

1865

c. 1869

loud round the fireplace. They were new and familiar, funny and sad, and were about things both ordinary and fantastic. "The Ugly Duckling," "The Little Mermaid," "The Princess and the Pea"—all these and more became beloved by children and adults alike. Hans knew that the best children's stories didn't talk down to their readers. Just like his parents used to encourage him, he used fairy tales to explore ideas that children may be unfamiliar with, but always from a point of view they could relate to. To Hans, fairy tales were "universal poetry"—anyone could love them, no matter their background. And he was right: his stories have been translated into 125 languages, and inspired countless plays and films. Today, he finds new fans with every generation, proving that while every tale has to end, imagination lasts forever.

Want to find out more about **Hans Christian Andersen?**

Have a read of these great books:

Hans Christian Andersen's Fairy Tales retold by Naomi Lewis

The Little Mermaid and Other Fairy Tales illustrated by Minalima

Brimming with creative inspiration, how-to projects, and useful information to enrich your everyday life, Quarto Knows is a favorite destination for those pursuing their interests and passions. Visit our site and dig deeper with our books into your area of interest: Quarto Creates, Quarto Cooks, Quarto Homes, Quarto Lives, Quarto Drives, Quarto Explores, Quarto Gifts, or Quarto Kids.

Text © 2020 Maria Isabel Sánchez Vegara. Illustrations © 2020 Maxine Lee-Mackie
Original concept of the series by Maria Isabel Sánchez Vegara, published by Alba Editorial, s.l.u
Produced under trademark licence from Alba Editorial s.l.u and Beautifool Couple S.L.

First Published in the UK in 2021 by Frances Lincoln Children's Books, an imprint of The Quarto Group.
100 Cummings Center, Suite 265D, Beverly, MA 01915, USA.
T +1 978-282-9590 **www.QuartoKnows.com**
All rights reserved.

No part of this publication may be reproduced, stored in a retrieval system, or transmitted, in any form, or by any means, electrical, mechanical, photocopying, recording or otherwise without the prior written permission of the publisher or a licence permitting restricted copying.

A CIP record for this book is available from the Library of Congress.
ISBN 978-0-7112-5934-8
Set in Futura BT.

Published by Katie Cotton • Designed by Karissa Santos
Edited by Katy Flint • Editorial Assistance from Alex Hithersay
Production by Nikki Ingram

Manufactured in Guangdong, China CC102020
1 3 5 7 9 8 6 4 2

Photographic acknowledgements (pages 28-29, from left to right) 1. HANS CHRISTIAN ANDERSEN (1805-1875) Danish author and poet painted by Christian Jensen in 1836 © Pictorial Press Ltd / Alamy Stock Photo 2. Hans Christian Andersen, 1845. Artist: Hartmann, Carl (1818-1857) © Photo by Fine Art Images/Heritage Images/Getty Images 3. Hans Christian Andersen in 1865 © Photo by Culture Club/ Getty Images 4. Hans Christian Andersen (1805 – 1875) Danish author © GL Archive / Alamy Stock Photo

Collect the Little People, BIG DREAMS™ series:

FRIDA KAHLO

ISBN: 978-1-84780-783-0

COCO CHANEL

ISBN: 978-1-84780-784-7

MAYA ANGELOU

ISBN: 978-1-84780-889-9

AMELIA EARHART

ISBN: 978-1-84780-888-2

AGATHA CHRISTIE

ISBN: 978-1-84780-960-5

MARIE CURIE

ISBN: 978-1-84780-962-9

ROSA PARKS

ISBN: 978-1-78603-018-4

AUDREY HEPBURN

ISBN: 978-1-78603-053-5

EMMELINE PANKHURST

ISBN: 978-1-78603-020-7

ELLA FITZGERALD

ISBN: 978-1-78603-087-0

ADA LOVELACE

ISBN: 978-1-78603-076-4

JANE AUSTEN

ISBN: 978-1-78603-120-4

GEORGIA O'KEEFFE

ISBN: 978-1-78603-122-8

HARRIET TUBMAN

ISBN: 978-1-78603-227-0

ANNE FRANK

ISBN: 978-1-78603-229-4

MOTHER TERESA

ISBN: 978-1-78603-230-0

JOSEPHINE BAKER

ISBN: 978-1-78603-228-7

L. M. MONTGOMERY

ISBN: 978-1-78603-233-1

JANE GOODALL

ISBN: 978-1-78603-231-7

SIMONE DE BEAUVOIR

ISBN: 978-1-78603-232-4

MUHAMMAD ALI

ISBN: 978-1-78603-331-4

STEPHEN HAWKING

ISBN: 978-1-78603-333-8

MARIA MONTESSORI

ISBN: 978-1-78603-755-8

VIVIENNE WESTWOOD
ISBN: 978-1-78603-757-2

MAHATMA GANDHI

ISBN: 978-1-78603-787-9

DAVID BOWIE

ISBN: 978-1-78603-332-1

WILMA RUDOLPH

ISBN: 978-1-78603-751-0

DOLLY PARTON

ISBN: 978-1-78603-760-2

BRUCE LEE

ISBN: 978-1-78603-789-3

RUDOLF NUREYEV

ISBN: 978-1-78603-791-6

ZAHA HADID

ISBN: 978-1-78603-745-9

MARY SHELLEY

ISBN: 978-1-78603-748-0

MARTIN LUTHER KING JR.

ISBN: 978-0-7112-4567-9

DAVID ATTENBOROUGH

ISBN: 978-0-7112-4564-8

ASTRID LINDGREN

ISBN: 978-0-7112-5217-2

EVONNE GOOLAGONG

ISBN: 978-0-7112-4586-0

BOB DYLAN

ISBN: 978-0-7112-4675-1

ALAN TURING

ISBN: 978-0-7112-4678-2

BILLIE JEAN KING

ISBN: 978-0-7112-4693-5

GRETA THUNBERG

ISBN: 978-0-7112-5645-3

JESSE OWENS

ISBN: 978-0-7112-4583-9

JEAN-MICHEL BASQUIAT

ISBN: 978-0-7112-4580-8

ARETHA FRANKLIN

ISBN: 978-0-7112-4686-7

CORAZON AQUINO

ISBN: 978-0-7112-4684-3

PELÉ

ISBN: 978-0-7112-4573-0

ERNEST SHACKLETON

ISBN: 978-0-7112-4571-6

STEVE JOBS

ISBN: 978-0-7112-4577-8

AYRTON SENNA

ISBN: 978-0-7112-4672-0

LOUISE BOURGEOIS

ISBN: 978-0-7112-4690-4

ELTON JOHN

ISBN: 978-0-7112-5840-2

JOHN LENNON

ISBN: 978-0-7112-5767-2

PRINCE

ISBN: 978-0-7112-5439-8

CHARLES DARWIN

ISBN: 978-0-7112-5771-9

CAPTAIN TOM MOORE

ISBN: 978-0-7112-6209-6

HANS CHRISTIAN ANDERSEN

ISBN: 978-0-7112-5934-8

STEVIE WONDER

ISBN: 978-0-7112-5775-7

MEGAN RAPINOE

ISBN: 978-0-7112-5783-2

MARY ANNING

ISBN: 978-0-7112-5554-8

MALALA YOUSAFZAI

ISBN: 978-0-7112-5904-1

ACTIVITY BOOKS

STICKER ACTIVITY BOOK

ISBN: 978-0-7112-6012-2

COLORING BOOK

ISBN: 978-0-7112-6136-5

LITTLE ME, BIG DREAMS JOURNAL

ISBN: 978-0-7112-4889-2